WHALES & DOLPHINS

A PORTRAIT OF THE ANIMAL WORLD

Andrew Cleave

TODTRI

This book was designed and produced by
Todtri Productions Limited
P.O. BOX 572
New York, NY 10116-0572
Fax: (212) 695-6988

ISBN 1-880908-20-4

Author: Andrew Cleave

Publisher: Robert M. Tod
Book Designer: Mark Weinberg
Editor: Mary Forsell
Photo Editor: Natasha Milne
Design Associate: Jackie Skroczky
Typesetting: Command-O,NYC
Printed and bound in Singapore by Atomic Press Pte Ltd

INTRODUCTION

The position of the ear of this bottle-nosed dolphin can be seen in a small pit behind the eye. Hearing is quite important in dolphins, which communicate with each other by means of a variety of sounds, some of them being clicks audible to humans.

It is 6:30 on a summer evening. The sun is still warm and reflected in a mirrorlike sea. A short way offshore in the deep channel separating a rocky island from the steep cliffs of the mainland, a shoal of mackerel breaks up the calm reflections in a frenzy of boiling water as they chase small fry to the surface. Suddenly, curved black fins slice through the mackerel shoal as a school of bottle-nosed dolphins arrive to catch the fish, repeatedly cutting through the shoal, their glistening black backs shining in the evening sunlight.

A flock of gleaming white gannets spots the turmoil in the water and over twenty of the large birds plunge-dive for the mackerel in the midst of the feeding dolphins. For several minutes the feeding frenzy continues as mackerel pursue small fry, and gannets and dolphins pursue the mackerel. Then, without any warning, a tall black fin, dwarfing the short, curved fins of the dolphins, breaks the surface and moves rapidly toward the intense feeding activity. The massive black-and-white back of a male killer whale, or orca, breaks through the boiling water, scattering dolphins and gannets, and then disappears as quickly as it appeared.

Twice more the fin emerges from the water, followed by the bulk of the powerful body, and then it is gone, disappearing as quickly as it came. The mackerel shoal vanishes, the gannets fly off elsewhere in search of fish, and the dolphins put in no further appearances. The whole spectacle lasts only a few minutes, but leaves a deep and lasting impression.

Experiences such as this may occur only once in a lifetime for those who normally rely on words and pictures for their information about these superb creatures, but even to the seasoned observer, who frequently encounters whales and dolphins in their natural habitat, this type of observation can still be an inspiration. We cannot easily enter the world of the whale, but when it briefly enters our world by appearing at the sea's surface it invariably provides a memorable experience.

The humpback whale is bulkier in appearance than most rorquals. This mother and calf were photographed off the coast of Hawaii.

Bow-riding bottle-nosed dolphins often accompany boats, swimming over to them for a while, and then, when tired of the experience, swimming away again to resume their normal activities. From time to time they will roll over to look at the human watchers in the bows above.

CLASSIFICATION OF WHALES AND DOLPHINS

As the blue whale begins a dive and lifts its tail out of the water, the massive tail stock can be seen, showing the powerful muscles the whale uses when swimming.

Whales and dolphins are collectively known as cetaceans, the word deriving from both Greek and Latin roots, meaning simply 'whales'. The whales are divided into two main groups: the toothed whales, or odontoceti, and the baleen, or moustached, whales, known as the mysticeti.

Toothed whales all have teeth in some form. The teeth may be numerous and almost identical in both jaws, as in the killer whale; present in the lower jaw only, as in the sperm whale; or reduced to one or two teeth only, as in some of the rarer dolphins. Toothed whales have a single blowhole on top of the head, although there are separate nasal passages inside the head, but baleen whales have a double blowhole on top of the head. The largest toothed whale is the huge sperm whale, a deep-diving creature of the open oceans, and the smallest toothed whale is the porpoise, often found close to shore and in large harbours.

Baleen Whales

Baleen whales range in size from the blue whale at up to 99 feet (30 metres) long to the minke whale at just over 29

The upper surface of a humpback whale's tail fluke, seen just before a dive, is all black with a notched edge, and may measure 13 feet (4 metres) across. This is what provides the power to swim.

A group of fin whales off the Massachusetts coast shows the typical curved fins of this species. There is usually some variation in fin shape, allowing different individuals to be recognised. Fin whales sometimes cooperate when feeding, operating in small groups to drive fish into tight shoals.

feet (9 metres).

The baleen whales have no teeth; instead they have large comblike structures, called baleen, which hang down from the roof of the huge mouth to filter seawater and trap food. There are two blowholes on top of the head.

The right whales are so-called because they were considered to be the 'right' whales to hunt. They all feed in waters close to the shore and are slow swimmers, thus making them easy to follow in a small boat. Once harpooned and killed they floated, so they could easily be towed back to the shore, and then once on shore they provided a rich source of blubber, whale meat, and 'whale bone', or baleen.

One of the earliest fisheries for right whales was based in the Bay of Biscay, and it so seriously reduced their numbers that the whalers were forced to travel to Greenland and Baffin Bay to hunt the bowhead, where the same thing happened, so this species too suffered a serious decline. Right whales are bulky, rounded whales with huge heads and mouths occupying about one third of the body. The upper jaw is long and narrow,

Grey whales travel to warm waters to breed, but find their food in colder waters farther north. They favour shallow lagoons from which they can scoop mud from the bottom and filter their food, usually shrimp, worms, and shellfish.

with an arched shape to help support the long, slender baleen plates.

The California grey whale is a more slender animal than the right whales, and its head is far less bulky; the upper jaw is arched and narrow. Grey whales are a distinct mottled grey in colour, and the body is usually encrusted with patches of whale lice and barnacles, especially around the head. It was at one time called the "devil fish" because of the vigorous way in which it defended itself when attacked by the early whalers, yet today it will gently approach small dinghies full of whale watchers and even allow them to touch it.

The rorquals are the family of whales containing the largest of all living things. They range in length from 23 feet (7 metres) to around 99 feet (30 metres). All of the rorquals are streamlined in appearance and are fast swimmers. The jawline is fairly straight, and there are many throat grooves allowing the mouth and throat to expand enormously when feeding. Inside the mouth the baleen plates are fairly short. Five of the rorquals are rather similar in appearance, differing only in size. The largest is the blue whale, followed in descending order by the fin,

sei, tropical (Bryde's), and minke. The humpback is also a rorqual, but this is not such a streamlined animal; it is far more bulky, has extremely long white flippers, a strange, knobbly head, and a smaller number of throat grooves. It is also more active at the surface than the other rorquals and frequently found near to the shore—characteristics that made it easier to hunt than the other whales, so it became very rare by the beginning of the twentieth century.

The tropical whale (Bryde's) is confined to the world's warmer waters, and is often seen lunge-feeding on fish shoals. It is similar in appearance to the large sei whale, reaching a length of up to 46 feet (14 metres).

The minke, or piked, whale has a ridge along its pointed snout and a straight jawline. Even when seen underwater, the large white patches on its fins show up very clearly, making this, the smallest of the baleen whales, an easy whale to identify.

Toothed Whales

Toothed whales have no baleen, but they do have recognisable teeth in some form or other, and they all seek fairly large prey, ranging in size from small fish and squid, to giant squid, large tuna and salmon, and even other marine mammals and whales.

The largest toothed whale is the sperm whale, both feared and sought after by the early whalers, and still a prey species today. Its lower jaw is dwarfed by the size of its enormous bulbous head with its curious single blowhole on the left side. Sharp teeth are found in the lower jaw, but none are present in the upper jaw. These teeth were a prize for the old whalers, who carved intricate designs on them on long winter nights, or during quiet times on whaling trips, producing an interesting form of art known as scrimshaw. This extraordinary creature is capable of the deepest and longest-lasting dives of any whale, and sadly for it, it provided some of the most useful materials for the whalers in the form of oils and fats, a rich flesh, and the so-

Humpback whales use a technique called lunge feeding to catch herring and krill.

Killer whales often breach, leaping almost completely out of the water. This gives whale watchers an excellent opportunity to photograph the markings of the whale so that it can be recognised if seen again. The breaching may continue for long periods, and one breaching whale is sometimes joined by several others.

called ivory from the teeth. The oil from sperm whales kept the lamps burning in large areas of the United States during the whaling boom of the nineteenth century.

One of the most well known of all whales is the strikingly marked killer whale, or orca. Males have a splendid upright dorsal fin, which can be over 6 feet (1.8 metres) tall, and both sexes are boldly patterned with black-and-white patches and a variable grey saddle behind the dorsal fin. Killers have sharp teeth in both jaws and these are used to grasp and tear up their prey, which can be anything from large fish to other marine mammals.

Pilot whales are large, sociable dolphins, reaching a length of up to 20 feet (6 metres). They are almost completely black, except for some grey markings behind the

eyes and dorsal fin, which is set fairly well forward on the body. They live in large schools at times, feeding on deep sea fish and squid, but they sometimes come so close to shore that they become stranded on beaches. This schooling habit and the tendency to come near to the land has led to thousands being slaughtered every year in Newfoundland, and especially the Faroe Islands, where they are driven into narrow inlets and butchered with long hooks and knives by the local inhabitants.

The beluga whale is unusual in being all white. Its bulbous head is separated from the body by a distinct flexible neck, and there is no dorsal fin. Adult males can reach a length of 16 feet (5 metres), but females are usually slightly smaller. Belugas live in groups of ten to twenty adults and

The striking, streamlined black-and-white head of the killer whale makes it easy to identify; pilot whales and melon-headed whales have all-black heads.

Female and juvenile killer whales have much shorter dorsal fins than the males, and they are also more strongly curved. They often swim in mixed groups, especially when hunting.

Belugas only rarely appear above the surface, and they are far less likely to breach than other whales. They sometimes come into such shallow water that they are in danger of stranding, but if left alone they usually manage to get back into deep water on the next high tide.

Short-finned pilot whales live in small schools, sometimes joining together to form groups of several hundred. They show the forward-positioned dorsal fin and muscular bodies typical of the pilot whales.

The beluga whale can be identified by its colouration, extremely flexible neck, and absence of a dorsal fin.

Pacific white-sided dolphins are wide-spread throughout the cooler regions of Pacific Ocean, usually avoiding the tropics. They sometimes get caught in gill nets set for large fish like tuna and salmon when they themselves are fishing underwater.

The bottle-nosed dolphin has a very distinctive hooked dorsal fin, which may show scars and notches if the dolphin is several years old and has been involved in fights with rivals or attacks by predators.

young, but come together in large schools of several hundred when on migration. They are confined to the Arctic regions where they feed on fish, sometimes in very shallow water. They make curious trilling calls when hunting, and are themselves hunted by native hunters each year. Their coastal habits make them vulnerable to oil spills, pollution, and disturbance by boats.

Beaked whales live in the open sea and feed on squid deep in the ocean. Their teeth are mostly reduced to one or two pairs; this helps them to catch their principal food of squid. The beaked whales have bulbous heads and a long, tapering snout, which gives them their name, and they all share one characteristic: a pair of grooves on the throat. Their bodies are compact and muscular, and the fins are small when compared with those of other small whales. Some species can reach a length of over 33 feet (10 metres), but very little is known about the biology of these strange creatures.

Dolphins are slender, streamlined small whales, and most species have well-developed snouts, pointed teeth, and recurved dorsal fins. They often live in large schools and are very active at the surface of the sea. Many species will bow-ride ahead of a boat and will often jump repeatedly out of the water in the hundreds. Some species are still fairly common and distributed throughout the world, but often end up in

The bottle-nosed dolphin has a pronounced snout and a set of pointed teeth, ideal for capturing the fish and squid it may find by echo-location.

drift nets set for other species.

Porpoises are the smallest of the whales, usually compact and plump with more rounded faces than the dolphins. Their teeth are more flattened and peglike and arranged in twenty-three pairs. Some porpoises lack a dorsal fin, but when it is present it is triangular, and never recurved as in the dolphins, so if the only part of the porpoise to show above the water is the fin it is not easy to tell which way it is swimming. Most species are less than 7 feet (2 metres) long when fully grown. Tens of thousands of porpoises are killed every year by fishermen, and some species are now endangered.

Common dolphins sometimes live in schools numbering hundreds, and when they all come to the surface together the water turns white with spray.

Schooling behavior among cetaceans ensures the mutual protection and survival of all members of the group. It also makes feeding easier, as shoals of fish can be 'herded' into tighter formations.

LIFE IN THE WATER

Whales and dolphins are highly specialised mammals adapted to live entirely in water, and yet, like humans, they must breathe air. Although some are able to dive to great depths, some live in icy cold polar seas, and some can find food where no light penetrates, they must all make regular trips to the surface to breathe. For most people, this will be the moment when they catch their first glimpse of a whale or dolphin. There may be the explosive blow of a great whale like the humpback followed by the curve of the broad back, or the sudden appearance of a curved black fin slicing through the water as a dolphin bow-rides ahead of a small boat, making short breaks in the surface with its small head to expose its blowhole to the air. The streamlined body may look fishlike, perhaps resembling a large shark, but the creature is definitely a mammal like us. Whales are warm blooded, they breathe air, they give birth to live young, and the mother suckles these on milk produced in mammary glands. They also have large, well-developed brains, which we are only just beginning to understand.

Skin and Blubber

Unlike most other mammals, whales do not have a body covering of hair, as this would hinder their progress in the water,

After lunging to the surface and capturing a shoal of fish, the humpback whale sinks back into the water, closes its mouth, and strains the water through its baleen plates, trapping thousands of fish in its mouth.

and despite their need for insulation in cold conditions they have a completely smooth and hairless skin. In order to maintain their high body temperature, whales have a thick insulating layer of blubber—a form of fat built up from the animal's food reserves.

The whale's body temperature is similar to ours, at around 99 degrees F (37 degrees C), yet it may be swimming in water below 50 degrees F (10 degrees C), and sometimes to the near-freezing point. Despite its very cold surroundings it is able to maintain this constant high body temperature.

A few cetaceans do possess some hair on their bodies. The rare and endangered right whale has a few hairs around its enormous mouth, and the similarly large bowhead whale has hair follicles on its head and snout. The snout of the humpback has a number of lumps on it which the old whalers used to call 'stove bolts', meaning rivets, because they looked as if they were there to hold the whale's head together. These are also hair follicles and may have some use as sense organs, possibly helping the whale to detect movements or the presence of its prey in murky waters.

Breathing

Whales must breathe air, and so they are forced to make regular visits to the surface to empty the stale air from their lungs and replace it with fresh air. As the whale breaks the surface the blowholes open and the characteristic spout, or 'blow', appears, sometimes accompanied by a loud rushing sound. This is the time when most large

The mighty blue whale is the largest animal ever to have lived on earth. Once it was found throughout the world's oceans, but now, after many years of persecution, it is a rare sight.

whales are first spotted; in the right conditions the blow can be seen from a great distance, and it usually lingers in the air for a few seconds.

The blow is actually water vapour that condenses in the cold air as it leaves the warmth of the whale's body. When a large whale surfaces after a long, deep dive, it will take several breaths before diving again, so there is usually an opportunity for whale watchers to study it for a short time. Normally a long dive is followed by a longer time at the surface. Many of the large whales that feed near the surface stay under for only a few minutes, but the record for long and deep dives belongs to the sperm whale, which can stay under for over an hour if necessary. In order to spend this length of time without breathing, it reduces the blood flow to certain parts of its body to save oxygen, and it has

the ability to store extra oxygen in its body tissues as well.

Swimming

Although whales and fish live in the same watery world, and they both swim through it, they do so with different body movements. Fish hold their tails vertically and move their bodies sinuously from side to side; their fins are used for balance and steering. Whales push themselves forward by moving their horizontal tails upward through the water. The forward thrust comes mainly from the upstroke of the tail, but some movement is also generated by the more gentle downstroke. Powerful muscles in the tail stock are used to move the tail up and down. When the tail of a species like the blue whale is seen out of water, the size of these muscles gives an indication of the power of the animal.

Killer whales spend a short time at the surface breathing before diving again in search of food. The blow of the killer whale is not as noticeable as its tall black dorsal fin, which is usually the first sign of its presence.

When a whale returns to the surface to breathe it empties its lungs with a loud rushing sound, and a column of water vapour, called the 'blow', rises into the air. The blow of the humpback whale is usually pear shaped.

25

Captured in the tranquillity of an Alaskan sea, the killer, or orca, whale emerges briefly from the water.

Small groups, or pods, of killer whales often swim into narrow inlets and sounds when following fish like salmon. They sometimes learn which are the best fishing spots and lie in wait for the fish to pass by.

The tail provides the drive, but the fins are used like the fins of a fish to steer and maintain a good balance in the water.

Diving

Well-built, buoyant whales like the right whales and humpback whales arch their backs and point their heads downward when starting a dive. As the body disappears the tail fluke emerges from the sea, water pouring off it, until it too finally slips beneath the surface; a sign that the whale has gone into a deep dive. The final sign is the fluke print, an oily-looking patch left on the surface that is caused by the swirl of the tail just below. The early whalers thought the whale was leaving a tiny oil slick behind as it dived, but it is really just a temporary disturbance in the water. The sperm whales, pilot whales, and some of the beaked whales dive to great depths, using powerful strokes of the tail to propel them downward, but other species, especially the plankton feeders, are nearly always fairly close to the surface.

A breaching humpback whale is a thrilling sight for whale watchers. This exciting behaviour, which is sometimes repeated many times, may be a form of communication, or a play activity in young whales.

With a loud crash, a killer whale breaches from the sea. In a moment's time, its body will clear the water.

When the whale begins a deep dive the head is pointed down and the tail comes up out of the water before finally disappearing after the whale, leaving only a swirl in the water.

Breaching

One of the most exciting spectacles any whale watcher can see is a huge whale leaping clear out of the sea. Several tonnes of sleek, black whale crashing onto the water with a mighty splash is a sight—and sound—never to be forgotten. Some species indulge in breaching more frequently than others. The large blue, fin, and sei whales hardly ever breach, but the humpback often does. The slow and ponderous right whale occasionally breaches, as do the grey whale and the deep-diving sperm whale. Breaching whales are popular attractions on whale-watching trips, and a challenge to photographers, but the breaching itself cannot be predicted; it often occurs just once without any warning and may not be repeated for several hours, but occasionally a whale will breach repeatedly, and may even be joined by others. Breaching is most common among humpbacks in their warm-water breeding grounds where there is a concentration of whales, so it is possible that it is used as a form of communication. Perhaps the whale that makes the loudest splash will appear stronger and more healthy to a prospective mate. If one whale breaches when others are within range, it is usual for another to breach soon afterwards. The huge splash, which can be heard several miles away, may be used as a warning, indicating to other whales that a particular area is already occu-

As the whale starts its deep dive it pushes its head down, arches its back, and shows its small hooked dorsal fin. The arched back seen at the surface is what gave the humpback whale its name; when it is swimming under the water its back is much straighter.

A small group of humpback whales lies quietly near the surface while one shows its tail in preparation for a deep dive.

When it breaks the surface, the pointed snout and the striped flanks of the common dolphin are clearly visible. The blowhole opens for it to breathe, but, unlike the large whales, there is no visible vapour from the blow.

The dorsal fin of the common dolphin is triangular in shape, with a slightly hooked tip, and it is set midway along the body.

Humpback whales have black-and-white markings beneath the tails, which are unique to each whale, enabling them to be recognised individually. This whale is an eight-year-old female called Circle who was spotted off the coast of Massachusetts.

Slender, smaller whales, dolphins tend to be very active near the sea's surface. They are also quite gregarious around people, swimming frequently ahead of boats.

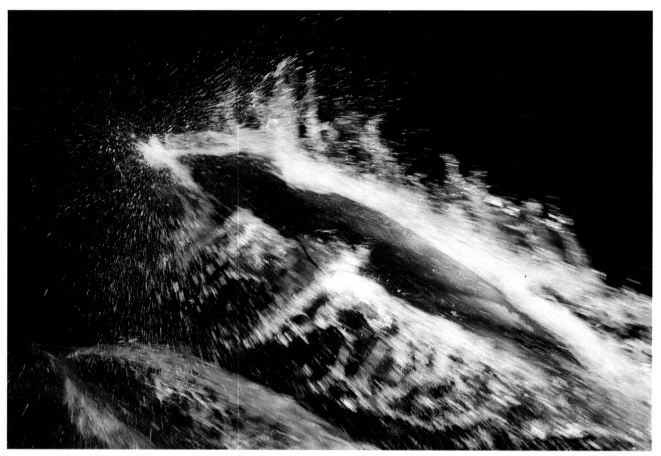

Dolphins propel themselves through the water with their powerful flukes, the flattened divisions of their tails. They steer with their pectoral fins and employ echo–location to navigate.

pied and they should keep away.

Breaching can take several forms. Humpbacks often emerge from the water on their sides, twist over with flapping flippers, and land with a splash on their backs. Most of the body clears the water, but the tail usually remains hidden. Occasionally a breach involves the whale landing on its belly, with its blowhole uppermost throughout the breach, enabling it to continue breathing.

Lob-Tailing and Flipper Slapping

Other lively surface activities frequently performed by humpbacks include lob-tailing and flipper slapping. A lob-tailing whale keeps the head and blowhole under the water while the tail is repeatedly slapped down on the water. This behaviour is sometimes used as a threat, as, for example, when a mother is guarding her calf and warns another whale to keep its distance. Flipper slapping is often observed

Dall's porpoises are lively and fast swimmers; when they break the surface they produce the well-known 'rooster tail' of spray, and they nearly always dash to a passing vessel to bow-ride, darting from side to side ahead of the bows with great skill.

The bottle-nosed dolphin is one of the most widespread dolphins in the world, and is often seen near the surface feeding on shoals of fish or bow-riding in front of a moving ship.

A breaching whale often comes out of the water on its side, rolling onto its back halfway through the breach, but sometimes it comes up with its belly uppermost and splashes down on to its back.

Flipper slapping displays sometimes involve the whale rolling onto its back and sticking both flippers out of the water before one or other of them is slapped down onto the surface.

when several humpbacks are feeding near each other. The whale turns on its side and slaps its long flipper on the water several times in succession. Occasionally it will roll on to its back and show both flippers above the surface, slapping one or other of them on the water. Sometimes these activities seem to be performed for the delight of a nearby boat filled with whale watchers!

Young whales are the most active breachers, and may start this activity only a few weeks after birth. This type of behaviour is unlikely to have anything to do with holding a territory or attracting a mate; it is more likely to be similar to the play activities seen in other young mammals when they engage in mock battles and chases,

and practise using muscles in preparation for the rigours of adult life when they will have to fend for themselves.

Spy-Hopping

A spy-hopping whale sticks its head vertically out of the water until the eye is exposed and then slips back down again without making a splash. This may be done to enable the whale to view the sea around it, possibly stimulated by the splash of a breaching whale elsewhere. Bowheads have been seen to spy-hop, but it is a common form of behaviour in grey whales, who will spy-hop alongside a small boat, dwarfing it and its human inhabitants, and then slip quietly back into the water with hardly a ripple.

Second in size only to the mighty blue whale, a fin whale, measuring up to 89 feet (27 metres) in length, shows its long back, broad snout, and the raised blowhole. Its hooked dorsal fin, which lies well back on the body, is not seen until the whale is about to dive.

The body of the grey whale is dark grey with lighter mottled patches, and it always has a heavy encrustation of barnacles and whale lice on it, especially around its head.

When first born, young grey whales are free from barnacles and whale lice, and the hair follicles on the rostrum can be clearly seen. The skin will soon begin to attract parasites, however, and the young whale will also receive many scars and other markings as it feeds on rough ground on the sea bed.

Dolphins always seem ready to interact with humans, and their complex language and apparent intelligence have long been the subject of study.

A distinctively marked tail of a humpback whale about to dive in very deep water close to the Alaskan shore. The whale may stay under for several minutes in search of food before returning to the surface to breathe.

The deep-diving sperm whale up-ends itself before commencing one of the deepest dives of all whale species. Once below the surface it may not reappear for over an hour, but it often comes up very close to the spot from which it dived.

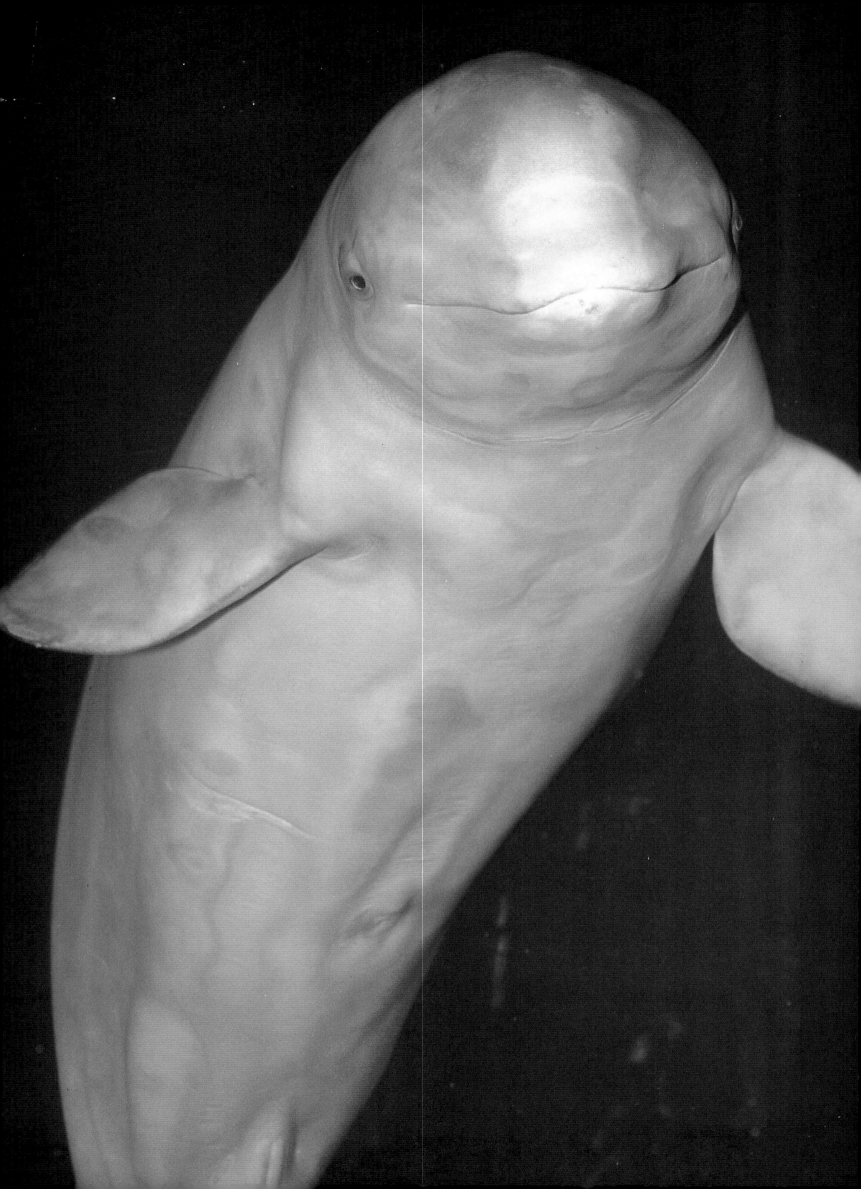

WHALE SENSES AND COMMUNICATION

The watery world that whales inhabit is different from ours in many ways, but one of the most important differences is that, except at the very surface, light does not penetrate it. Eyesight is therefore not very important to most species. Whales certainly do have a sense of sight, but it is not as vital to them as their sense of hearing and the ability to detect vibrations transmitted through the water. The colourings and markings of whales have more to do with camouflaging them in the uniform world they live in than in enabling whales to recognise each other.

Only a few of the dolphin species that spend most of their lives near the surface are at all colourful or strongly marked. The common dolphin and the striped dolphin have attractive markings, but many species, like the sperm whale and most of the toothed whales, are a uniform dark grey or black. The eyes of some of the large whales are very difficult to see, being dwarfed by the huge head, and they are usually set well back behind the jaws.

Hearing

Sound travels very well in water. A loud human cry may be heard up to half a mile (800 metres) away on land, but the call of a whale in the deep ocean may be detected 50 miles (80 kilometres) away. Some whales have developed an elaborate language using sounds that are audible to

A small group of spotted dolphins in the waters off the Bahamas seeks out fish. If the water is clear like this, they can easily see their prey, but at night or in cloudy water, they find it by echo-location.

The beluga has a very expressive face and a more flexible neck than most other whales, enabling it to turn its head independently of its body.

human ears. The humpback whale produces strange grunting and snoring sounds, but also makes a haunting and mournful cry. It seems to have quite a vocabulary, which it uses to produce 'songs' heard at the breeding grounds. Each whale sings its own distinctive song, which may last for an hour or more, and be repeated many times from its favourite singing position.

The white beluga whale was called the sea canary by the whalers in the past, who likened its twittering calls to the song of this bird. The calls are loud enough to be heard above the water, and when a large group is calling to each other the sound carries for quite a distance.

As well as producing audible (to humans) sounds, many whales produce high-frequency ultrasonic sounds in the form of short clicks, which they use for echo-location. The baleen whales are not thought to do this, but the sperm whale and many other toothed whales use this method. The bursts of sound are directed forward, and if they hit an object, the returning echo can

A small group of humpback whales in the deep waters off Point Adolphus, Alaska, show their arched backs, the first sign that they are preparing to dive. This area is a favourite feeding ground for humpbacks in summer, as it provides a rich supply of fish.

Bottle-nosed dolphins have powerful stream-lined bodies, making them skillful and fast swimmers. They are extremely agile underwater and are easily able to capture fast-swimming fish and squid.

be detected by the whale, giving it useful information about its surroundings. Prey can be located in total darkness by this method, and it is also possible to communicate with other whales with the aid of these sounds.

Touch, Smell, and Taste

The thick skin and the protective layer of blubber beneath the whale insulate the animal from its surroundings, making the sense of touch less important than in other mammals. Whales are aware of objects touching their bodies, and some species have a few sensitive hairs around the mouth, but tactile stimuli are generally not so important to them.

Smell and taste are rather poorly developed in whales and dolphins. Studies have shown that the part of the whale brain that deals with smell and taste is much smaller than in land-living mammals and is almost absent in the sperm whale and some of the deep-diving toothed whales. There are tastebuds in the tongues of some species, and captive dolphins have been shown to be able to detect the difference between some chemicals, but the overall conclusion is that

taste and smell are not very important to most whales.

Navigation

It is possible that some whales are able to navigate using the earth's magnetic field as a compass. Several species are known to have tiny fragments of magnetite embedded in tissues around the head and neck, and studies of fin whales have shown that they follow lines in the earth's magnetic field that run in a

A rolling fin whale shows the throat pleats that enable it to expand the size of its throat when feeding. Fin whales take small fish as well as tiny shrimp and usually feed near the surface.

The large, all-black bulbous head of the long-finned pilot whale cannot be mistaken for the black-and-white killer whale. The huge head contains a structure that helps the whale echo-locate squid and fish in the darkness of deep water.

Killer whales are found in all the world's oceans, even reaching the pack ice of Antarctica. These cold regions are often very rich in food, attracting many seals, so, despite the cold, the whales will find plenty of prey there.

The calf of the southern right whale rarely strays far from its mother in the first year of its life. Its body has very few barnacles and whale lice on it when it is first born, but as it grows older it acquires them, too, and ends up looking more like its mother.

north-south direction when they are on long migrations between the polar regions and the tropics. Little research has been done on this, however, and so no firm conclusion can be drawn as to how important this sense is or even if it is present in all whales and dolphins.

COURTSHIP AND MATING

The large baleen whales spend most of their lives alone or in very small groups, feeding in the vastness of the oceans, so finding a receptive member of the opposite sex for a mate can be very difficult, especially when the populations of some species have been reduced to a few thousand animals. However, most species of large whales make seasonal migrations to warm waters for the purpose of giving birth, and it is here that they form concentrations where males can find a mate. One group of humpback whales spends the months from November to March in the Caribbean, where single males sing their melancholy songs to attract females.

The males will approach any females

The 16.5-foot- (5-metre-) long flipper of the humpback whale, longer than the flippers of any other whale, is dark on the upper surface and white below, and sometimes encrusted with barnacles and whale lice. The scientific name of the humpback whale is <u>Megaptera</u>, meaning "long winged."

they encounter, most of which are accompanied by a small calf, and if not immediately rejected, will stay with them for about a quarter of an hour, during which time mating may take place. Sometimes another male will join the threesome and attempt to mate with the female. A great deal of jostling, head-butting, bubble-blowing, and grunting and trumpeting will follow as each male attempts to become the female's escort. This commotion can be heard for several miles around, so often a crowd gathers with up to fifteen males joining the group.

Occasionally the principal escort will be replaced, and several males may get the chance to mate with the female, but after a few hours the group disperses and the

A killer whale calf stays near its mother for several years, suckling on her rich milk and learning how to hunt. Even when old enough to fend for itself, it will still remain near its mother in the same social group into which it was born.

The young bottle-nosed dolphin will stay with its mother for at least a year, feeding on milk at first, and then gradually learning about different types of food by tasting scraps she leaves behind. Once mature it will stay in the same school.

Grey whales often 'spy-hop', rising vertically out of the water until the whole head can be seen. This may be done to enable the whale to see what other whales are doing, or it may simply be a form of display.

Common dolphins in the Sea of Cortez, Mexico, have sought out the warmer waters of the southern winter, which takes place between July and November.

The hooked dorsal fin of a female minke whale shows clearly as she prepares to dive, while her calf lunges out of the water beside her showing its white throat and clean, straight jawline.

Female spinner dolphins give birth to a calf every second or third year after a long gestation period, and they suckle their young for at least seven months. Adult spinner dolphins feed at night on fish and squid that rise to the surface when darkness falls.

After feeding near the surface, the blue whale rolls on to its side, showing the pleats that enable the throat to expand when food and water are taken in. This vast animal feeds on tiny shrimp called krill, which it needs in large amounts every day.

Right whales have short, blunt, all-black flippers, seen here as a whale rolls on its back. These help this slow-moving whale manoeuvre in shallow water.

whales all return to their original stations to continue singing. Similar activities occur when the southern right whales gather off Peninsula Valdes in Argentina during the southern winter between July and November, or when the grey whales gather in Magdalena Bay off the west coast of Mexico. For some of the rarer toothed whales and the species that live far from the shore in the open oceans, there are very few observations by humans, so their courtship and mating will probably remain a mystery for many years.

Giving Birth

Female whales give birth to a single calf that, when born, is very highly developed. In most of the large baleen whales, gestation lasts for about a year. In the sperm

whale gestation takes about sixteen months, and in some of the beaked whales, such as Baird's, it can take seventeen months. Newborn whales are fed on a rich milk and grow very rapidly; they may be suckling from their mothers for up to ten months, and by the time they are weaned they will have increased their weights by up to eight times. Young sperm whales may not be weaned for up to three years, and there are reports of female sperm whales up to seven years of age, and males up to thirteen years old, still suckling from their mothers from time to time.

The actual birth of a whale is rarely seen, but there are a few observations on some species. Studies of sperm whales off Sri Lanka showed that females give birth near to the surface and the young is born tail first. In order to be able to take its first breath, the newly born whale is helped to the surface by its mother and sometimes by a number of "aunts" waiting nearby. Sometimes an aunt will look after the baby sperm whale while its mother makes a long deep dive. The calf of the southern right whale has been observed staying very close to its mother for the first few months of its life, hardly ever straying more than a few body lengths from her side. The California grey whale's calf is also very closely tied to its mother, lying alongside her while she rests at the surface, and lolling across her head when she comes up to blow.

The calves are large in proportion to the size of their mothers when compared with the young of land living mammals. A baby porpoise may be forty percent of the size of its mother at birth; this large size is an adaptation to coping with the sudden cold it experiences when suddenly leaving the warmth of its mother's body for the cold of the open sea.

Whales at Rest

In order to breathe, whales must actively inhale and exhale. This is not an automatic process, as it is in other mammals. If a whale becomes unconscious it stops breathing and dies, so it is unable to sleep as we know it. Many species of whales are known to rest quietly at the surface, and it appears that they are 'daydreaming', with

Most humpback whales are all black above with some white markings on the tail and flippers, but this very unusual black-and-white humpback was seen near Adelaide Island, off the Antarctic Peninsula.

Photographed underwater, a pair of common dolphins swim together off the coast of Mexico. They are no doubt part of a larger school that feeds cooperatively.

one half of the brain shut down while the other half keeps them breathing.

It is sometimes possible to approach whales very closely while they are resting in this way, as they often seem to be far less aware of what is going on around them. They usually lie horizontally at the surface with just the blowhole and part of the top of the head exposed—a habit known as 'logging', This is often a time when the whale is hit by a fast boat that is not keeping a proper lookout. These bouts of logging may last for several minutes, and can take place in the middle of the day. Some whales even snore while they are logging; humpbacks can sometimes produce a resonant trumpeting sound that is surprisingly loud; when heard in the narrow confines of a fjord or deep valley it echoes around the surrounding hills.

Spotted dolphins are very variable in the amount of spotting they show, but young dolphins have very few spots at first.

FEEDING

It is a strange paradox that the largest of all living things feeds on some of the smallest of living things. Many of the largest baleen whales, such as the blue and right whales, are plankton feeders, taking vast quantities of small organisms ranging in size from microscopic plants to tiny shrimps. The toothed whales are mostly fisheaters, but some will take other creatures such as squid, crustaceans, and sea cucumbers. The killer whale takes fish, but some also prey on other whales, seals, and sometimes turtles and squid.

Spotted dolphins have a varied diet, feeding on several species of fish and squid. They usually hunt in groups, causing their prey to bunch together by attacking from all sides.

In order to be able to extract their small food items from sea water the large whales have developed an elaborate straining mechanism. The baleen whales have a row of horny plates hanging down from each side of the upper jaw. Along the edges of these plates are large numbers of stiff bristles that act like sieves. When the whale opens its jaws and gulps in a large mouthful of water, plankton and shrimp will be drawn in as well. Next, the mouth is partially closed, the tongue then wipes along the plates, scooping off the food particles, which can then be swallowed. The whole process takes only a few seconds,

The huge mouth of the humpback whale gapes open as it lunges to the surface in pursuit of a shoal of herring or capelin. After it has broken through the surface it will close its mouth and capture the fish, straining water out through its baleen plates.

A school of common dolphins makes an exciting spectacle as over twenty of them break the surface at once. For every dolphin breaking the surface there will be others under the water, so attempting to count them when they display like this can be very difficult.

Common dolphins are very fast swimmers and when they decide to race a vessel only the fastest boat can keep up with them, and they can easily out-manoeuvre a boat with quick twists and turns. They often leap clear of the water showing off the colourful markings on their flanks.

but it is repeated over and over again as the whale swims through its food-rich water, and is punctuated by trips to the surface to breathe. Although the principle is the same in all the large whales, the width and length of the bristles varies a great deal between the different species.

The grey whale has fairly short, coarse bristles, which it uses to strain mud scooped up from the bed of shallow seas. The mud contains small shrimp called amphipods, and these are strained out easily by the coarse baleen.

The mighty blue whale has baleen plates almost 3.3 feet (1 metre) long and these have very fine bristles along their edges to strain out

the very small shrimp it feeds on. These shrimp, called krill, sometimes occur in enormous numbers, making the sea look slightly pink from the air.

Many of the large whales, and especially the humpback, can be observed at the surface when they are lunge feeding. The whale lunges rapidly toward the surface with the jaws open and the throat pleats distended. On breaking the surface, the whale often lands with a splash on its side or belly, and sometimes on its back. Minke and tropical (Bryde's) whales also do this, and may engage in sideways rolls as well. The larger fin and sei whales often pursue fish with open jaws and end the chase with

Humpback whales often cooperate to feed on a large shoal of fish, driving it into a tight formation before all breaking through the surface together with their mouths wide open.

a sideways roll.

Humpbacks have evolved a unique method of catching fish called bubble-netting. Bubble-net feeding is used to make shoals of fish or krill easier to capture in large quantities. One or two animals will make a deep dive below the shoal and then spiral upward, releasing a stream of small air bubbles from the blowhole; these bubbles form a circular curtain in which the prey are trapped.

The sperm whale is the largest toothed whale and it feeds mostly on large squid, captured at great depths in the deep ocean. They may dive to as much as 6,600 feet (2,000 metres) below the surface and stay down over an hour at a time. At these great depths there is no light and the water is very cold, yet the whales are able to locate and capture their prey with ease. Some of the squid taken by the whales can be giants themselves and may be over 36 feet (11 metres) long.

The killer whale, or orca, is another well-known large toothed whale. It preys on fish like salmon, but will also take sharks,

seals, other small whales like dolphins and porpoises, and even, when hunting in pods, may attack the largest of all, the blue whale. Killer whales are highly social animals, living in well-organised social groups. Some groups are large and live within a fairly well-defined home range, but other are 'transients' and wander more widely in the oceans. The groups that live in one home range are more likely to have learned how to take one type of food very successfully, so they may well be fish eaters, but the wandering whales are more likely to attack seals or other whales as

they roam the oceans. Killers are found throughout the world's oceans, from icy polar regions to the warm waters of the tropics.

Many of the smaller dolphins are fish-eaters, and some will also take squid; they have rows of sharp teeth which enable them to capture and hold on to their prey. Some of the wide-ranging species like the bottle-nosed dolphin and white-sided dolphin have a very varied diet, taking whatever happens to be available. The dolphins often live in large schools, and when they locate a shoal of fish and start feeding the

Male killer whales have the tallest dorsal fins, usually about 6.5 feet (2 metres) high, and some individuals, especially older males, have a wavy margin to the fin, making them easier to recognise when in a group.

The striking silhouette of the long-beaked spinner dolphin, with its long snout and triangular dorsal fin, makes it easy to recognise when seen from a ship. This playful creature may repeat the leaps and spins over and over again and be joined by hundreds of others as well.

Remarkably agile, common dolphins appear to race each other through Pacific waters.

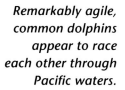

surface of the water can become white with spray as the panic-stricken fish break the surface.

The schooling dolphins and porpoises often cooperate to make feeding easier. They keep in touch with each other by means of sounds, and by visual contact, and then when a shoal of fish has been located they herd it into a tighter formation near the surface. The fish can then be picked off easily; from the surface, the water will appear to be boiling, and frightened fish will skim over the water in an attempt to escape. Some dolphins drive shoals of fish into shallow water near beaches before capturing their food.

CONSERVATION

In the early years of the twentieth century, whaling fleets were to be found in all the world's oceans and many nations had a whaling industry. That began to change after public opinion was roused by many

Spotted dolphins are very acrobatic, often leaping completely clear of the water. They may do this as a form of play or when escaping from a predator like a large shark or a killer whale.

Bottle-nosed dolphins are playful creatures and will often leap clear of the water. If trained in a dolphinarium, they will do this in response to a signal, or perhaps in return for a reward of food, but in the open sea they will do this at will, possibly just for fun.

The head of the southern right whale is encrusted with colonies of barnacles and whale lice, which form variously shaped patches in different individuals, enabling them to be recognised whenever seen. The blowholes point away from each other, giving rise to the characteristic forked blow of the right whale.

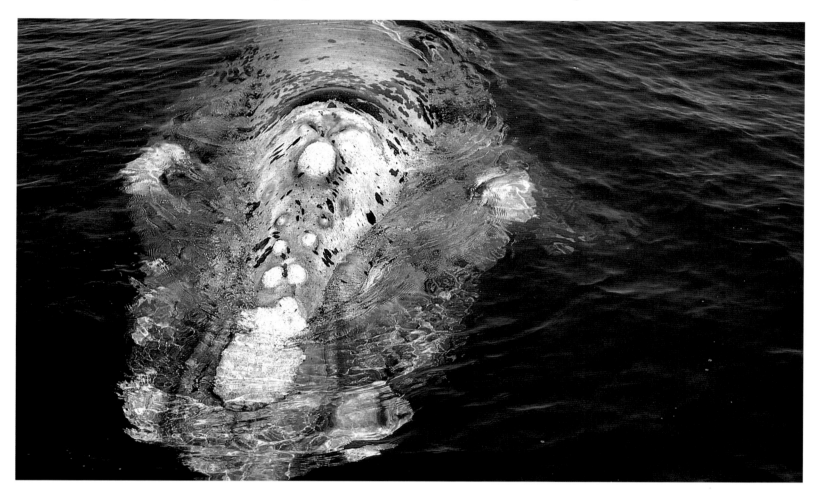

The blue whale, seen from the deck of a ship, really is blue. Its body is covered by tiny organisms that create a blue effect when seen underwater. Many blue whales actively avoid boats, remembering the days of whaling when they were hunted and harpooned.

conservation bodies, most notably Greenpeace, who pursued the whaling fleets with the same vigour with which they pursued the whales. Horrific films were shown on television news broadcasts of the way in which the whales were slaughtered, and statistics were published revealing how drastically the populations of the whales had crashed.

Recordings were made of the song of the humpback whale and played on radio and television around the world. The public was moved by the haunting and melancholy sounds they heard and realised that these creatures were warm-blooded mammals like them, with brains, with feelings,

and with a right to live the oceans free from the horrors of modern commercial whaling.

Many nations, such as the United Kingdom and the United States, stopped whaling in the 1960s, and the International Whaling Commission (IWC) set quotas for the remaining whaling nations in an attempt to safeguard the dwindling stocks of whales left in the oceans. Some species, such as the humpback, were given full protection, while others, such as the sperm whale, which were thought to be in less immediate danger of extinction, were given more limited protection.

By 1982, however, a complete ban on commercial whaling was agreed by the IWC, and by 1986 no whale species could legally be hunted for commercial gain. Some nations protested, most notably Japan, Iceland, and Norway and continued hunting whales for so-called scientific reasons. Several thousand whales were slaughtered during each year of the ban, many of the carcasses ending up in Japan to be sold for human consumption. By 1992, some of the whaling nations decided to break away from the IWC to form their own body and begin commercial whaling once more. During the years of the ban, the whaling fleets continued to patrol the oceans and kill some whales, and it seems likely that the slaughter will resume.

The threats to whales are many and some are very serious. Apart from the dangers to

The bottle–nosed dolphin is among the unfortunate species that can become accidentally entangled in fishermen's nets.

The bodies of whales and dolphins, like this bottle-nosed dolphin, are often covered with scars and scratches. These may be the result of encounters with predators like sharks or killer whales, or the result of fights between rivals of the same species.

Dall's porpoise is one of the smallest cetaceans, reaching a length of just over 6.5 feet (2 metres) when fully grown. They are easily recognised by their small size, black-and-white markings, and triangular dorsal fin.

The markedly hooked dorsal fin of the Pacific white-sided dolphin gives it its other name of hook-finned porpoise. It often leaps clear of the water and seems to be unconcerned about the presence of boats nearby. A single dolphin like this is unusual as they normally live in large schools.

In the long twilight of a summer evening in Alaska, humpback whales will continue feeding and diving all day, making use of the rich food supplies of the Arctic summer.

them of commercial and 'scientific' whaling, many whales and dolphins die in fishing nets set for other species, or are slaughtered by commercial fishermen who see the whales as a threat to their own interest. Tuna fishing involves setting enormously long drift nets, which entangle tuna fish, the object of the exercise, but also ensnare dolphins, sea lions, turtles, albatross, and many other innocent forms of marine life. Some of the nets, which can be thousands of meters long, become so heavy with carcasses of dead dolphins and other creatures that they sink to the sea bed. Once there the carcasses slowly decay and disintegrate, and when they have broken up, the net is free to float to the surface again where it may catch even more innocent creatures until, as before, it becomes so heavy that it sinks to the sea bed once again.

Some species of whales have reached the verge of extinction and may never recover to their normal population levels, while many others are in danger of reaching the same situation. The sea-going nations of the world cannot agree on measures to save the remaining whales and dolphins; while they argue, more and more of these magnificent creatures are dying, not just through deliberate acts of slaughter, but as a result of pollution and entanglements as well. It would be a sad reflection on this generation, if, knowing what we know now about the problems facing whales, we fail to take the necessary action to save them for future generations.

The Pacific white-sided dolphin has up to twenty-eight small pointed teeth, typical of all the dolphins, in each jaw which it uses to help it feed on squid, anchovies, and hake.

Engaged in vocalising a series of sounds that are part of the complex system of dolphin communication, this animal appears to be laughing.

The Pacific white-sided dolphin has a short, thick beak, strongly marked in black, and a gleaming white underside.

The long-beaked spinner dolphin is found in the warmer parts of the eastern Pacific Ocean, where it sometimes occurs in schools of over one thousand and can provide one of the most exciting spectacles for travellers at sea.

A breaching humpback whale is an unforgettable sight—as well as an opportunity to observe the animal's characteristic throat grooves and long flippers.

The tall fin
of the male
killer whale
slices through
the water in
the calm of
a summer
evening.
This is one
of the most
easily recog-
nised of all
whales and
can be seen
in most of the
world's oceans.

As one whale
dives after
breathing, its
blow disperses
in the cold air
of an Alaskan
morning, but
it is quickly
joined by the
blow of a second
whale swimming
alongside it.

PHOTO CREDITS